The Hofstra Adventure

The Story of
An Emerging University

CLIFFORD L. LORD

"Were American Newcomen to do naught else, our work is well done if we succeed in sharing with America a strengthened inspiration to continue the struggle towards a nobler Civilization— through wider knowledge and understanding of the hopes, ambitions, and deeds of leaders in the past who have upheld Civilization's material progress. As we look backward, let us look forward."

—CHARLES PENROSE
(*1886-1958*)
Senior Vice-President for North America
The Newcomen Society
for the study of the history of
Engineering and Technology
(*1923-1957*)
Chairman for North America
(*1958*)

This statement, crystallizing a broad purpose of the Society, was first read at the Newcomen Meeting at New York World's Fair on August 5, 1939, when American Newcomen were guests of The British Government

"Actorum Memores simul affectamus Agenda"

This Newcomen Address, dealing with the history of

Hofstra University, was delivered at a National Meet-

ing of The Newcomen Society in North America held

"It was a singular act of boldness and courage to start a new college in the pit of the Great Depression with just a large house, 15 acres of land and no endowment. It was almost rash, an act of derring-do, and as such set a significant precedent—often followed—in the later history of the school. Those executors, in this first great decision in Hofstra's history, showed that willingness to take a calculated risk that has been characteristic of Hofstra's leadership time and time again over the years."

—CLIFFORD L. LORD

        ℧   ℧

The Hofstra Adventure

The Story of An Emerging University

CLIFFORD L. LORD, Ph.D.,
LL.D., L.H.D.

MEMBER OF THE NEWCOMEN SOCIETY
PRESIDENT
HOFSTRA UNIVERSITY

THE NEWCOMEN SOCIETY IN NORTH AMERICA
NEW YORK   DOWNINGTOWN   PRINCETON   PORTLAND
1970

Copyright, 1970
CLIFFORD L. LORD

❦

*Library of Congress
Catalog Card Number: 71-120177*

❦

*Permission to abstract is granted
provided proper credit is allowed*

❦

*The Newcomen Society, as a body,
is not responsible for opinions
expressed in the following pages*

❦

First Printing: December 1970

❦

SET UP, PRINTED AND BOUND IN THE UNITED STATES
OF AMERICA FOR THE NEWCOMEN SOCIETY IN
NORTH AMERICA BY PRINCETON UNIVERSITY PRESS

INTRODUCTION OF DR. LORD AT NEW YORK CITY ON MARCH 26, 1970, BY MR. BERNARD FIXLER, PRESIDENT, CREATIVE MAILING SERVICE, INC., GARDEN CITY, CHAIRMAN OF THE BOARD OF TRUSTEES, HOFSTRA UNIVERSITY, MEMBER OF THE NEW YORK COMMITTEE IN THE NEWCOMEN SOCIETY IN NORTH AMERICA

My fellow members of Newcomen:

IT is scarcely surprising that when the Trustees of Hofstra University were casting about for a president they set out to find a dynamic, enterprising, innovative type of candidate. And, it is to the Trustee's lasting credit that they also required that this person be deeply and personally involved in the humanities and, in particular, that he be sincerely human and warm in his relations with his fellowmen. The splendid and ever-growing reputation of Hofstra University has proven conclusively that the Trustees did their work well when they agreed that Dr. Clifford Lord should be Hofstra's president.

That was in 1964. Since then, Cliff Lord has made a deep and lasting impact upon the burgeoning population of Long Island. He has taken a deep interest in all phases of community life and Long Island will long remember his vigorous and successful efforts to help disadvantaged members of our society to achieve an education.

His leadership has produced a growing student body and one with even higher scholastic standards. New buildings to house the increasing activities appear on the Hempstead Plains with regularity. A new School of Law, the first in New York State in 45 years, is Hofstra's latest contribution to the educational growth on Long Island. His enthusiasm has brought together an unusually talented faculty. His ventures into innovativeness have brought forth New College with its individual contributions to each of its students.

These qualities and talents were a result of much hard work on the part of Dr. Lord in the field of education. Born in White Plains, New York, he earned his B.A. and M.A. at Amherst College. This was followed by his Ph.D. at Columbia University. Later, he served on the faculty of Columbia on two occasions—the latter as Dean of the School of General Studies and Professor of History. In between these appointments, he directed the New York State Historical Association and started the famed Farmer's Museum at Cooperstown. His work in directing the State Historical Society attracted national attention.

He served with the U. S. Navy during World War II and while in uniform co-authored a *History of U. S. Naval Aviation*. His work in the field of history continues through his many publications which appear regularly. In spite of the almost impossible administrative load he imposes upon himself, he still finds time to get acquainted with literally hundreds of Hofstra students. It is this tremendous capacity for work, blended with a genuine consideration for all students on the campus which make Hofstra University the quality institution it is.

It gives me great pleasure to introduce to you the President of Hofstra University, DR. CLIFFORD LORD.

My fellow members of Newcomen:

THE years since World War II have seen in this country the establishment of an extraordinary number of new colleges—many public, many sectarian, and quite a few private non-sectarian institutions.

Spurred, in various combinations, by the G.I. Bill of Rights, a tide of higher expectations, the urge for maximum social mobility, one of the great periodic waves of egalitarianism of American history, and the technical demands of an increasingly complex and affluent society and economy (in which the machine—including the computer—did more and more of the work), young men and women in record numbers and record proportions finished high school and went on to some form of higher education. The extraordinary names on the decals in the rear window of the student car and the unfamiliar institutions listed on the sports pages on autumnal Sunday mornings, bear witness to the rash of new colleges founded in recent years. For the last decade or so, they have been a-borning at the rate of one a week. Since we are all conscious of this phenomenon, and many of us have sons and daughters at some of these newer institutions, it may be useful to spend this evening on the story of one of these colleges, now a small university: one which got started a bit earlier than most in this boom, and one which has done rather better than most of its newcomer peers.

Every institution has its own flavor, its own aura, its own distinction. The Hofstra story goes back to April 6, 1933. Under the buoyant leadership of Franklin Delano Roosevelt, the New Deal is in full flower: NRA, AAA, SEC, TVA, HOLC, PWA, CCC, FERA—friends of our childhood, all. The sick chickens who killed General Johnson's Blue Eagle—in one of the most stunning form reversals of all time—will not come home to roost via the Schecter case for six more weeks. Social Security, the National Labor Relations Act, WPA, and the CIO will come into being before the year is out. The Dow-Jones Index stands at 59 for industrials, 19 for utilities. Unemployment has been reduced from fifteen million to twelve and one-half. Apples are still selling on major Manhattan street corners, and the widowed Kate Mason (Mrs. William S.) Hofstra, has just executed a new will. It will be probated before the year is out.

Her husband, a genial and hard-headed millionaire of many interests, including a lumber and a paper company in Hempstead, had died two years earlier. After providing trusts for a daughter by a previous marriage and two grandsons, he had left all his personal property and the residue of his substantial estate to his beloved Kate. Childless herself, the widow Hofstra left specific gifts to friends and the Metropolitan Museum of Art, provided for her housekeeper and her twenty-three cats, and asked that the residue "be devoted to a public charitable purpose." She named James H. Barnard and Howard S. Brower, the latter her husband's partner in the lumber business, as her executors. It would be agreeable to her if the house and its surrounding 15 acres were to be used by the Masons, of which her husband had been an active member, as a lodge or a public park, as a memorial to William S. Hofstra.

The estate was somewhat remote from the center of town. A large house and fifteen acres of land to maintain without an endowment had little appeal to the Masons in the heart of the Great Depression. They declined. The executors talked of a nursing home, then finally of a college.

The latter was the brainchild of Dr. Truesdale Peck Calkins, former Superintendent of Schools of the Village of Hempstead, and at the moment, Director of the Bureau of Appointments of New York University. He had long had a vision—a college in the middle of rapidly growing Nassau County. Here was the chance. He talked to his friend, Howard Brower. Reputedly, the decision was made one day as the executors and Calkins rode the Long Island Railroad into the city. It would be a college, a branch of New York University, a memorial to their friend, William S. Hofstra.

So there came into being "Nassau College-Hofstra Memorial," an extension branch of NYU. NYU furnished the faculty, established the curriculum, ran the operation. A young and reportedly exciting faculty—all of them instructors, except Dean Arthur D.

Whitman—took on the first entering class of 159 day students and 621 evening students. Tuition was $375 per year. It was September 1935.

It was a singular act of boldness and courage to start a new college in the pit of the Great Depression with just a large house, 15 acres of land and no endowment. It was almost rash, an act of derring-do, and as such set a significant precedent—often followed—in the later history of the school. Those executors, in this

THE TOWER OF HOFSTRA'S LIBRARY SOARS ABOVE THE HOFSTRA HOME, NOW HOFSTRA HALL, WHERE THE UNIVERSITY HAD ITS GENESIS.

first great decision in Hofstra's history, showed that willingness to take a calculated risk that has been characteristic of Hofstra's leadership time and time again over the years.

Elements of the future University took shape at once. The day program featured the liberal arts. In the afternoons and evenings, the NYU Schools of Education and Commerce gave courses to part-time students in teacher training and business. These were the three main curriculum areas from that day to this.

The original plan had been for a two-year program at Hempstead, with those qualified moving to the main NYU campuses for the last two years of undergraduate work. Satellite or feeder systems are not unknown in higher education. There are often difficulties, and the situation at Hofstra Memorial was no exception.

Students used to commuting to the relatively nearby Hempstead campus did not relish the prospect of commuting daily to the city. It would be not only an inconvenience and a waste of time, but a substantial extra expense (and the Depression was still on). A four-year program was agreed upon, but other problems remained. Was a faculty, all of the rank of instructor, even though three had their Ph.D.'s, adequate to the task? Or was NYU exploiting the Hofstra situation by "cheap labor," depriving the Nassau students of a quality education? The venture looked financially promising. Construction of Brower Hall, the first building on the first of three quadrangles designed by Aymar Embury, architect and master planner of the Hofstra campus for 27 years, produced a net deficit of $70,000 for the first year of operation, but daytime enrollment the second fall more than doubled, while the evening enrollment remained steady. When profits began to show, would NYU drain them off to the city?

Reportedly, the discussions at times were acrimonious. In any case, the NYU Council agreed to a separation in mid-December, 1936, a mere fifteen months after Nassau College opened, and on January 19, 1937, the Regents granted a provisional charter to Hofstra College.

Dr. Calkins became first President of the College, and Howard Brower, Chairman of the new Board. Under a two-year transitional arrangement, the new Board had financial control, NYU retained academic control until 1939. The first two graduating classes (1939 and 1940), entered when the College was part of NYU, were given the choice of a Hofstra or an NYU degree— and a surprisingly large majority chose a Hofstra diploma, indicative of the early esprit of the campus.

THE UNISPAN BRIDGES THE EIGHT-LANE HEMPSTEAD TURNPIKE WHICH SEPA-RATES THE NORTH AND SOUTH CAMPUS.

State law required resources of $500,000 before a college could be given a permanent charter, and in January, 1940, Trustee Brower turned over to the College $700,000 from the residuary estate of Kate Mason Hofstra (another $100,000 came later). Hofstra College received its absolute charter on February 16, 1940. By this time, there were five buildings, athletic fields, and a campus of 25 acres. Daytime enrollment had risen that fall to 697. The campus newspaper and yearbook, local social fraternities, a student government and the usual roster of extracurricular activities were in full swing.

William S. Hofstra had been born in Holland, Michigan, and was proud of his Dutch ancestry. He had called his big home "The Netherlands." Under President Calkins, the Dutch "heritage" of Hofstra College became firmly implanted. The alma mater of the new College was put to the music of the Dutch national anthem. The College Seal, with royal permission, was taken from the Seal of the House of Nassau. The student honor society was called Bovenaan. Ambassador Loudon in April, 1940, presented a Netherlands flag with a Hofstra seal. Ties with the Holland Society have been maintained. The ROTC Color Guard since 1966 has worn the uniforms of 17th century Dutch Burgher Guards. Teams were nicknamed "The Flying Dutchmen."

Outside events now intervened disastrously in the affairs of the fragile young College. On September 1, 1939, Nazi Germany invaded Poland. Nine months later, after the lightning-like Panzer campaigns, Poland had been partitioned, Norway, Denmark, Belgium, Luxembourg occupied. The British had evacuated the Continent at Dunkirk and Vichy France had signed an armistice. Two months later, the mass bombing of British cities began. In September, Japan invaded Indo-China, and on October 17, American men registered for Selective Service for the first time since World War I.

Civil Aeronautics Administration courses in flight training had been introduced at Hofstra the year before. Now came short courses to train technical personnel for defense work, together with various emergency service and management defense training courses. As the male part of the student body dwindled rapidly, the faculty taught one summer session (1942) without pay to help tide over the growing financial emergency. Teaching loads became unpredictable, as many young faculty left in mid-semester for the armed services, government jobs, or defense industry.

Mounting financial problems, as the student body shrank and the faculty disappeared, proved too much for Dr. Calkins, who died of a heart attack, June 8, 1942, aged 64. Trustee Brower took over as acting president and served for over two years. Beginning with the fall of 1942, varsity sports were suspended for the duration. Students commuted on "B" gasoline ration cards. Early one morning in March, a plane from Mitchel Field Air Force Base, lying immediately north of the then-campus across the Hempstead Pike, crashed into Barnard Hall. The pilot was the only human casualty, but next day the campus lost 99 of the beautiful trees in which William Hofstra had taken great pride, cut down by Air Force personnel.

The coeds were also leaving, going into nursing, defense industry, and the armed services. By the fall of 1943, the women's registration was only two-thirds of normal, while the men were down to one-sixth the pre-war figures. Faculty and staff forewent salary increases. Book purchases were suspended. Brower Hall was closed for the duration.

The situation was desperate. The deficit for 1941-42 alone was $21,868, and shortly thereafter the Trustees decided to give up the fight and close the College. But this required the consent of the chartering body, the Regents. Brower went to Albany. The Commissioner of Education heard him through, then, with staff, visited the campus. Then came the second critical decision in the Hofstra adventure, a decision forced upon the Trustees. The validity of Calkin's dream of a college in the heart of burgeoning Nassau County was affirmed. The College would be very much needed when the war was over, the troops came home, and the defense industries returned to normal. But how to keep it solvent in the meanwhile? Would the Trustees take Robert Moses on the Board? Of course. So the fiery Commissioner joined the Board,

EACH SPRING, HOFSTRA'S UNIQUE REPLICA OF THE GLOBE THEATRE STAGE IS INSTALLED IN THE PLAYHOUSE FOR THE ANNUAL SHAKESPEARE FESTIVAL.

logically announced that he could have nothing to do with raising money because of conflict of interests with his public positions.

But in the next two (of 13) years on the Board, Robert Moses performed two major services for the institution, in one of the less known chapters of his distinguished career. He chaired the Postwar Planning Committee, which resolved that the College should acquire all nearby land as it became available, drop all evening and graduate work, and get a new President. He also chaired the Committee to select the new President, and was responsible for bringing Dr. John Cranford Adams, distinguished young Shakespearean scholar from Cornell, to a notable 20-year term as second President of Hofstra.

President Adams took office August 1, 1944. The previous spring the entire Student Council was composed of coeds, and two women were added to the Board. Under the new administration, the pickup was immediate, as Dr. Adams ordered a number of studies in preparation for the postwar years. The war in Europe ended nine months later, May 7, 1945. The war in the Pacific ended three months later, August 14th, a year after Dr. Adams took office. The G.I.s came home, and the G.I. Bill sent those who wanted to go to college. It was one of the most remarkable and memorable college generations of all time. None of us who taught or knew them will forget the tremendous motivation, the maturity and purposefulness of these returning young veterans. They came to Hofstra in substantial numbers—ultimately (February 1957) hitting a high enrollment of 2,646—and ushered in a new era.

The number of students on campus in the fall of 1945 was still well below that of the immediate pre-war years. But by the following fall, all records were broken: 1,672 full-time day students (1,313 of them veterans); a freshman class of 1,065, vis-à-vis a previous high total enrollment of 731 full-time students. Four years later, the total enrollment was doubled—more than 3,500. The campus was put on a double schedule. An evening branch was opened in Hempstead High School. Quonsets were erected temporarily on campus.

In accordance with the recommendations of the Moses Committee, the physical limits of the campus were expanded. A tract to the west gave the College Holland House for the Presidential offices and a Board Room. Twenty-five acres south of the campus gave a new site for the athletic fields. Later the East Campus was acquired, where the Stadium, Field House and Computer Center were built. In 1948, the purchase of a relatively small tract brought the total campus to 59 acres. And 13 new Embury buildings were added to the campus year by year, their cream-colored powdered brick, their Georgian style, grouped around three quadrangles, no building more than two stories high because of the adjacent air base, producing a handsome cream and green, cloistered campus. Outstanding were the Playhouse, the Lowe Arts Building, and Memorial Hall—a dining and meeting, or student center, facility.

Admissions were selective from the outset. Through 1947, the student graduating in the top quarter of his class was admitted automatically; those in the second quarter took an aptitude test, those in the third and fourth quarters took "such tests as the Admissions Committee required." Beginning in 1948, the Herman-Nelson Test of Mental Ability and the Nelson-Denny Reading Test were required of all applicants, as well as selected vocational and personality tests. A number of schoolmen were put on the early Boards, giving Hofstra an edge (I wonder) in getting the best students graduating from those school systems. And the limited scholarship funds were awarded, especially in the first (Depression) years, to high school valedictorians and salutatorians who would come to Hofstra. Attention was first paid to Scholastic Aptitude scores—that bane of all parents of contemporary high school students—in 1958. In that year, the profile of our freshman class nationally stood at the 50th percentile.

In 1945-46, the war over, intercollegiate athletics were resumed: basketball for 1945-46, baseball for the spring of 1946, football for the fall of 1947, wrestling (a new sport at Hofstra) for 1946-47.

In 1949, the curtain rose in Calkins Gymnasium on the first annual Shakespeare Festival. Dr. Adams, whose intensive doctoral study had made him the country's prime authority on the Globe

Theater, supervised the construction of a dismantable scale replica of its multi-faceted stage, which—later transferred to the new Playhouse—has been the unique attraction of the annual Festival ever since. Currently, the Festival lasts two full weeks, with performances of a Shakespeare play three evenings and a Sunday matinee each week; special daily afternoon performances for and by high school students; a second period play, madrigals, and other special features.

A particularly strong Drama Department was developed during the Adams presidency, which continues to shed lustre on the whole institution. Equally strong was the History Department, with other special strengths visible in psychology, biology, economics, and throughout the humanities and social sciences. A decision, primarily for financial reasons, not to go beyond the undergraduate level in engineering and the hard sciences inhibited development in these areas. Library collections numbered 35,136 books by 1950; passed the 100,000 mark in 1957; presently number over 400,000. The MS in Education and the MBA degrees were added in 1951, along with the two-year Associates degree in Arts and Applied Sciences in an abortive attempt to head off community college competition in Nassau County. This was also the year (1951) in which, for the first time in some years, evening enrollment passed day-time in number of bodies. This condition was to prevail for some 15 years.

The Korean War and the seeming correlation during World War II between the presence on campus of ROTC programs and a college's ability to secure contracts for special wartime training programs, prompted the administration to apply successfully for an Army ROTC unit for the campus in 1951. The McCarthy era produced an amendment to the Faculty Statutes declaring Communists ineligible for appointment. "Urbanity" was likewise a quality expected of the professoriate. Though racial or religious admissions quotas had never been tolerated at Hofstra, the first Trustees of Catholic and Jewish persuasion (one each) were elected to the Board in 1958; student and faculty delegates (2 each) were added in 1969; the first blacks (2) in 1970.

Expansion of the campus was financed on a pay-as-you-go basis, with short term loans for particular buildings carried by the

SINCE THE MAJORITY OF UNDERGRADUATES STILL COMMUTE FROM LONG ISLAND
HOMES, THE STUDENT CENTER LOUNGES ARE AN ESSENTIAL TO THEIR ON-CAMPUS
SOCIAL LIFE.

Meadowbrook Bank (now the National Bank of North America). When the Playhouse, largest and most costly unit built up to that time, was erected in 1958, Augustus B. Weller, President of the Meadowbrook Bank and long-time Trustee of the College, recognizing the value to the College of involving some of his fellow bankers in the development of this burgeoning institution, tried in vain to start a consortium of other Long Island banks to finance this and future Hofstra projects. Among the 600 institutions receiving special grants from the Ford Foundation for the improvement of faculty salaries, Hofstra in 1956 received $522,200, the earnings on which were to be used for faculty salary enhancement. The result was that Hofstra salaries jumped to preeminence on the Island, which helped greatly in maintaining the high calibre of the faculty until eroded by the major inflation of the period of the Vietnam War and the competition of the public (tax-supported) institutions. Primarily this was an era of great prosperity, of the G.I. Bill of Rights, of an enormous expansion of higher education across the country, and Hofstra prospered accordingly.

The last two years of Dr. Adams' long presidency were plagued with illness, but they witnessed two more major decisions, both of them milestones in the Hofstra adventure. The first was the decision to apply to the Regents for University status; the second was to go residential and take on a long-term debt for further development of the campus.

The decades of the 50's and the 60's were a period of changing nomenclature in higher education. Normal Schools had become Teachers Colleges, now became colleges and in some instances universities. Some liberal arts colleges even initiated doctoral programs but retained the collegiate name. Overgrown liberal arts colleges with a few graduate programs became universities. Hofstra was one of the latter. The catalytic agent apparently was the reported intention of nearby Adelphi College to become a University. Hofstra moved first. The University designation received Regents' approval February 7, 1963. Perhaps to potential donors "university" would sound more prestigious than "college" and so spur the drive to raise sorely needed funds to match a Ford Foundation Challenge grant (one million dollars if Hofstra—which had never dreamed of raising any such sum—raised two million). To the Trustees, the change presupposed an extension of the Masters programs, then numbering 17, the beginning of doctoral work, and the possibility of graduate schools. The new "university" consisted of two colleges (1) Hofstra College, with five Divisions: Humanities, Social Sciences, Engineering and Physical Sciences, Education, and Business and (2) an experimental freshman year program (also Ford Foundation sponsored) somewhat euphemistically labelled "New College," for which a separate 50-acre campus at Old Westbury was obtained. In the College, Engineering, Education, and Business potentially could be developed into separate schools with graduate programs. Education promptly was, and won early professional accreditation. There were now 22 buildings on a campus of 77.2 acres, to which 88 acres of Mitchel Field (declared surplus by the government) had just been added, an endowment of $3,144,136 (cash value); 3,743 full-time and 5,077 part-time students.

The second major decision of the closing months of the Adams regime was to ask for $11,450,000 in State Dormitory Authority bonds to finance a major expansion of the campus, involving a sorely needed new Library, a bridge across the Hempstead Pike to those newly acquired 88 acres of Mitchel Field and the erection on North Campus of a new Student Center and the initial resi-

ON-CAMPUS HOUSING FOR 1,500 STUDENTS IS AVAILABLE IN MODERN TOWER DORMITORIES.

dence halls of the heretofore commuter college. The need for both Library and Student Center was transparent; but existing facilities were sorely overcrowded. The decision to go into residence halls was based on population projections which showed that the number of Nassau and western Suffolk County high school graduates admissible to Hofstra would plateau in the late 1960's and not increase again until the middle 1980's. With Nassau Community College coming into being on Mitchel Field itself with ambitious plans to become a very large four-year college, a huge State University Center planned for Stony Brook just over the Suffolk County border and only 40 miles away, and a second major State University four-year college planned for Westbury only 12 miles

[19]

away, the Board faced the prospect of lowering admissions standards and the calibre of the entering classes at Hofstra or broadening the geographic base of its student recruitment. The latter meant dormitories, and the Trustees opted for dormitories. So the new University undertook the first long-term (30 year) debt in Hofstra's history.

Meanwhile, the first big fund-raising drive, the Ford Challenge Fund grant, after two rather languid years, finally went over the top just before midnight on the last day of the drive. Had it not been for the indefatigable efforts of a handful of men, particularly the then-Chairman of the Board, Daniel L. Monroe, and the then-Director (now Vice President) for Development, Luis Bejarano, the drive would have failed utterly.

As President Adams retired at age 62, due to ill health, the stage was thus set for a new administration, that of the present incumbent. Hofstra now boasted an attractive campus, fully paid for; a first-rate undergraduate faculty, unusually devoted to the College; no debt or mortgage except that very recently undertaken for the expansion of facilities; a growing (local) reputation; a student admissibility attracting growing attention from guidance counsellors in the metropolitan area; trustees, alumni, faculty, friends just finished with their first major experience in fund-raising; an organized and functioning development office with imaginative leadership.

Lack of time to achieve historical perspective on the past six years, as well as the speaker's deep personal involvement, interdict any but the sketchiest suggestion of recent developments.

Of great significance was the fifth major decision of the Hofstra adventure, the decision of a highly conservative Board, October 5, 1965, to take out a second State Dormitory Authority bond issue for an additional $14,860,000. The then-Board, recruited on the understanding that they would not have to raise money, confessed its disinclination and unreadiness to undertake another big fund drive. It would restructure itself, recruit members with more financial clout, and meanwhile—so as not to lose momentum in restructuring the campus to meet the on-coming public competition—would borrow more money. Two more residence halls were

involved, the life sciences center, the first phase of a physical
fitness and health research center which attracted the endorsement
of the President's Committee on Physical Fitness (and widespread
interest among insurance companies, among others), an addition
to the recently completed Student Center. It was another magnifi-
cent calculated risk. Momentum was preserved, facilities greatly
improved, and a new Board recruited.

The new University quickly converted New College into a
degree-granting branch with a three-year innovative curriculum.
This fall New College became a four-year college by adding a
"year of encounter" (in Harlem, Appalachia, an Israeli kibbutz),
i.e., a year's structured learning experience in an unfamiliar milieu.
The Division of Business became the School of Business, inaugu-
rated an innovative and successful MBA thesis program, stressed
decision-making, economics, theory and ethics in place of the older
nuts-and-bolts courses, and, in 1969, was given professional accreditation. The Evening Program became University College.
The program in elementary education was completely revamped,
as well as practice teaching in the School of Education, while
special education (for the severely handicapped) and an experi-

RAMPS ARE PROVIDED THROUGHOUT THE CAMPUS AND BUILDINGS ARE ACCESSIBLE
FOR PHYSICALLY HANDICAPPED STUDENTS CONFINED TO WHEELCHAIRS.

mental Nursery School were added to the program. The promise of Oceanology led to the establishment, with Town cooperation, of a research facility at Point Lookout, with County cooperation at Sheeps' Meadow, and participation in an interinstitutional research facility at Montauk. In the College, the so-called "house plan," though houseless, has made a frontal intellectual, and to some extent social, attack on the facelessness of the individual in an entering freshman class of 1,100. The facilities of the new Library encouraged the introduction of 4-point advanced courses involving heavy reading assignments; experimental combinations of reading instruction with courses requiring substantial readings, as in history; independent study programs; eleven new Masters, and the first four doctoral programs. Degree requirements for the baccalaureate were liberalized to give the undergraduate student, beginning next fall, far greater latitude in tailoring his individual curriculum (with faculty advisement) to his individual needs. The academic enterprise was enhanced by the rapid building up of the Library, including notable gifts such as that of the Paul Radin collection in anthropology and ethnology; by the increasingly sophisticated equipment of the Computer Center; by the recent two million dollar pledge to develop our Library resources in the fine arts. Distinguished academic figures have been added to the bevy already gracing the faculty: Leon Charney and Frank Griffith in Education; Stanley Young, Colin Turnbull, Louis Lomax in the liberal arts; Leo Barnes in Finance; David Kadane and Eric Schmertz, the first two appointees to the faculty of the new Law School; Ellsworth Mason, distinguished Joyce scholar and Director of Libraries, are examples.

Centers for Business and Urban Research and for Research in Aging, Bureaus of Educational Studies and Services, and of Educational Evaluation (with Ford Foundation support), have been established. The profile of the entering freshmen has risen in ten years from the initial fiftieth decile, already cited, to the eighty-third. The Hofstra Players' performance last year of *Rashomon* was chosen to open the first American College Theater Festival, sponsored by the Smithsonian Institution, in Washington, last April. The Repertory Theater was invited that same year to the Yale Spring Drama Festival while its year's program

INVITING STUDENTS TO DO INDEPENDENT STUDY AND RESEARCH, THE IN-
TERIOR OF THE UNIVERSITY LIBRARY WAS DESIGNED WITH A WARM AND
INFORMAL DECOR.

was videotaped for national distribution by ETV. Hofstra students
have won far more of the coveted Woodrow Wilson and Danforth
Fellowships than the students of any other Long Island institution. Professional fraternities in Education, Business, and Management were admitted to the campus. So, also, on a trial basis, were
national social fraternities.

Hofstra's reputation as an innovative institution brought it not
only international recognition—it was, for instance, one of the
seven American institutions selected by Dr. Earl McGrath, former U. S. Commissioner of Education, to be included in his study
of educational innovation in colleges and universities in the western world—but charter membership in the select and stimulating
Union for Research and Experimentation in Higher Education.
The first new law school to be opened in New York State in 45
years opened at Hofstra this fall. The Internal Revenue Service brought its North Atlantic Training Center to Hofstra, to add

interchanges, particularly in faculty, with the graduate program in the School of Business and in the School of Law, to the cluster of related graduate programs we are evolving in business, education, law, and the social sciences. University governance was restructured to give maximum autonomy to the individual academic units, under over-all University standards and guidelines effected by a University Senate. This is now under review by a blue-ribbon committee on which students, faculty and administration are equally represented, attempting to adjust the present power structure at Hofstra to the universal demands for major student participation in the governance of their colleges and universities. Two student delegates already sit with the Board of Trustees and the University Senate, 24 sit with vote with the University faculty. Student Advisory Councils meet with several deans and other top administrators, and in a number of departments. Student government has broad authority over student affairs.

The availability of residence facilities, coupled with proximity to two major airports, made Hofstra an attractive site for conferences with an international flavor, such as the international conference sponsored by the French-Polyclinic Hospital on the ideal medical center for the year 2000. The University became the eastern port of entry for high school students from Europe coming through the American Field Service, for a year's study in this country. It became an eastern center for debriefing of various foreign visitors—Iranian mayors and others.

Five years ago Hofstra launched the professional Hofstra String Quartet, which last year appeared in a special program before the New York State Music Association. A year later, the University started the first professional symphony to be resident on an American campus, a unique opportunity for music majors and others. The Pro Arte was of sufficient quality to attract, in 1968, the distinguished Eleazar de Carvalho from the St. Louis Symphony to be its musical director and permanent conductor.

In the identification, non-partisan discussions and solutions of community problems, Hofstra has taken an advanced role, beginning twelve years ago when it staged, on a non-partisan platform, a debate about labor-management relations which set, for at least a decade, a new atmosphere for labor-management relations on Long Island.

Three more tracts on Mitchel Field were added to the campus, bringing the total to 227 acres. The student body rose to 13,000. Seventeen more buildings were added to the physical plant, nearly tripling the campus floor space. Hofstra, with the first outdoor installation of AstroTurf in the East, became the summer training

EVENING CLASSES ARE AN IMPORTANT PART OF HOFSTRA AND THE CAMPUS IS BRIGHTLY LIGHTED.

center for the Jets. The Flying Dutchmen were joined by the Rolling Dutchmen (wheelchair student basketball team).

ꙮ ꙮ

This administration began in a buoyant economy. It is now confronted with its share of the basic problems of our society and economy: (1) the social revolution with all its implications for higher education and for the institution which is the leader of its community in this university-centered era; (2) the continuing inflation which is posing a major threat to the continuance of private higher education; (3) the drug-culture and our relationship to them and theirs to us; (4) student discontent, ranging from those legitimately unhappy about war, poverty, hypocrisy, the despoliation of the planet and eager to do something constructive about it, to those so alienated as to seek only the revolutionary destruction of the present system and "establishment."

And so, Hofstra, leader for its area (Long Island), with a budget of over $20,000,000 a year, a $50,000,000 plant and a $7,000,000 endowment, has emerged as one of the quality *new* schools and *the* emerging young University of the metropolitan area, in the new university-oriented society and economy. This has been the result of many factors:

(1) the tradition of the calculated risk, first adopted by the founding fathers, a key part of the dynamic and rational flexibility of this vibrant young institution which is so tangibly and visibly on the move.

(2) the emphasis from the outset on quality—quality of students; quality of faculty; the quality reflected by the many prizes won by the Library and the other new buildings; the quality impulse reflected in going for AstroTurf instead of sod, or in the stature of our Pro Arte Symphony.

(3) a long-standing willingness to innovate—witness New College, the "houseplan," the MBA thesis program, the major curriculum reforms in the College, Education, and Business; the novel curriculum of the new Law School; our pioneering programs for the culturally disadvantaged and the physically handicapped; the Board's adoption of an "adventurous" investment program.

(4) the insistence from the beginning of the institution that, while encouraging research and publication and giving these accomplishments due weight in promotion and annual raises, its faculty must be primarily a teaching faculty. In short, before most, it cared, it does "give a damn."

(5) the increasing assumption of University responsibility for the identification and resolution of the problems of its

immediate and its larger community, especially the social revolution, in which Hofstra has predated its peers in many particulars and programs.*

(6) an insistence that students govern themselves to the outer limits of their willingness responsibly to govern themselves, and a willingness to accept and expand student freedoms if the students will effectively accept the responsibilities which accompany those freedoms.

(7) the emergence of our "older" alumni—the first of whom graduated from Hofstra less than thirty-one years ago—now, or recently, White House advisors, presidents of small and middle-sized corporations and banks, vice presidents of the larger corporations and banks; distinguished public servants; well-known actors, entertainers and motion picture directors; professors of distinction, academic administrators at all levels, including one university president; a baker's dozen *bona fide* millionaires.

The Hofstra of today is a function and product primarily of the men and women—students, faculty, alumni, administrators, trustees, friends—who have married the institution and devoted lives and substance to its development. It is a lively, dynamic place. It is a friendly place. It is a place of quality.

ଔ ଔ

It has been a happy function for me, tonight, to give you this cursory insight into the history of one of our many newer colleges and universities, into the inter-relationship of its history with the history of the nation, into the administrations of the first two presidents which prove again that our institutions are so often the lengthening shadows of their heads.

I close with two suggestive quotations.

The first comes from the late lamented *New York Herald-Tribune* of April 1, 1965: "If Hofstra University can achieve in the next thirty years what it has in the past three decades, it could be one of the world's leading institutions of higher learning."

* *Hofstra and the Social Revolution*, by Clifford Lord, 1970, Hofstra University, a separate.

The second, from the oral critique following a three-day traditional visit by, in this case a very prestigious team, from the Middle States Association of Colleges and Universities. It began with the dean of a well-known eastern institution saying, "I wish I could bottle up some of the èsprit and élan of this campus—faculty, students, administration—and take it home with me. You have it and we do not."

Not too many years ago, young alumni were sometimes confronted with the supercilious question "What is a Hofstra?" This has changed. More typical today is the sports page of the *Los Angeles Times*, Friday, October 17, 1969. The day before (in the presence of my wife and myself) the Amazing Mets had won the World Series to become, unexpectedly, the World's Champions of organized baseball. The full page headline in the *Los Angeles Times* was: "Mets Make Believers of the Orioles and the World." The lead sentence was, "Now all I have to live for is to see Hofstra in the Rose Bowl."

THE END

❦

"Actorum Memores simul affectamus Agenda!"

THE NEWCOMEN SOCIETY
in North America

I N APRIL, 1923, *the late L. F. Loree (1858-1940) of New York, then dean of American railroad presidents, established a group now known as "American Newcomen" and interested in Material History, as distinguished from political history. Its objectives center in the beginnings, growth, development, contributions, and influence of Industry, Transportation, Communication, the Utilities, Mining, Agriculture, Banking, Finance, Economics, Insurance, Education, Invention, and the Law—these and correlated historical fields. In short, the background of those factors which have contributed or are contributing to the progress of Mankind.*

The Newcomen Society in North America is a non-profit membership corporation chartered in 1961 under the Charitable Law of the State of Maine, with headquarters on North Ship Road, Uwchlan Township, Chester County, Pennsylvania, some five miles east of Downingtown, Pennsylvania, and 32 miles west of the City of Philadelphia. Here also is located The Thomas Newcomen Memorial Library in Business History, a reference collection, including microfilm, open to the public for research and dealing with the subjects to which the Society devotes attention.

Meetings are held throughout the United States of America and across Canada at which Newcomen Addresses are presented by leaders in their respective fields. These manuscripts represent a broadest coverage of phases of Material History involved, both American and Canadian.

The approach in most cases has been a life-story of corporate organizations, interpreted through the ambitions, the successes and failures, and the ultimate achievements of those pioneers whose efforts laid the foundations of the particular enterprise.

The Society's name perpetuates the life and work of Thomas Newcomen (1663-1729), the British pioneer, whose valuable contributions in improvements to the newly invented Steam Engine brought him lasting fame in the field of the Mechanic Arts. The Newcomen Engines, whose period of use was from 1712 to 1775, paved a way for the Industrial Revolution. Newcomen's inventive genius preceded by more than 50 years the brilliant work in Steam by the world-famous James Watt.

The Newcomen Society in North America is affiliated with The Newcomen Society for the Study of the History of Engineering and Technology, with offices at The Science Museum, South Kensington, London, S.W. 7, England. The Society is also associated in union with the Royal Society for the Encouragement of Arts, Manufactures and Commerce, whose offices are at 6 John Adam Street, London, W.C. 2, England.

ꙮ   ꙮ

Members of American Newcomen, when in Europe, are invited by the Dartmouth Newcomen Association to visit the home of Thomas Newcomen at Dartmouth in South Devonshire, England, where the festival of "Newcomen Day" is celebrated each year on the fourth Friday in July.

❦

"*The roads you travel so briskly
lead out of dim antiquity,
and you study the past chiefly because
of its bearing on the living present
and its promise for the future.*"

—LIEUTENANT GENERAL JAMES G. HARBORD,
K.C.M.G., D.S.M., LL.D., U.S. ARMY (RET.)
(1866-1947)

*Late American Member of Council at London
The Newcomen Society
for the study of the history of
Engineering and Technology*

❦